On Abducting the 'Cello

By the same author

Man in a Window, 1965 (Coach House Press)
Eighteen, 1966 (Coach House Press)
For Everyone, 1967 (Fleye Press)
Music for the Words, 1967 (privately printed)
The Machinery, 1967 (privately printed)
Alphabook, 1972 (Makework Press)
Glass/Passages, 1976 (Oberon Press)
An Ache in the Ear: 1966–1976, 1979 (Coach House Press)
The sea us (with bpNichol) (unpublished)
Mirages, 1996 (privately printed)

On Abducting the 'Cello

Wayne Clifford

The Porcupine's Quill

National Library of Canada Cataloguing in Publication

Clifford, Wayne, 1944–
On abducting the 'cello / Wayne Clifford.

ISBN 0-88984-237-x

I. Title.

PS8555.L53505 2004   c811'.54   c2004-900233-3

Published by The Porcupine's Quill, Erin, Ontario.
www.sentex.net/~pql

Readied for the press by Eric Ormsby; copy edited by Doris Cowan.
Interior photographs are by Mary Joan Edwards.

Represented in Canada by the Literary Press Group.
Trade orders are available from University of Toronto Press.

We acknowledge the support of the Ontario Arts Council and the
Canada Council for the Arts for our publishing program. The financial
support of the Government of Canada through the Book Publishing
Industry Development Program is also gratefully acknowledged.
Thanks, also, to the Government of Ontario through the Ontario Media
Development Corporation's Ontario Book Initiative.

 Canada Council
for the Arts

Conseil des Arts
du Canada

 Canadä

 ONTARIO ARTS COUNCIL
CONSEIL DES ARTS DE L'ONTARIO

for Rilke's musty funnybone,
and for my Victoria and John Gray,
wherever they went

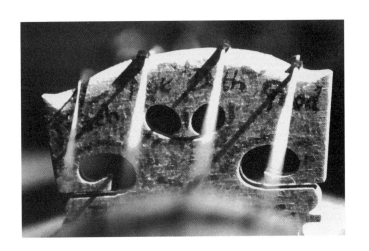

*(A Prologue,
establishing our protagonist's credibility
by way of the pennywhistle.*

A woman pausing at her sink remarked:
'Those nickel-plated rhythms might relieve
an nth part of my chores. Would you believe
how they could be applied?' The piper barked
down the empty bore he played so badly.

'Lady,' he replied, lifting his lips
around the whistle, 'this penny's worth's what slips
a little ease between us. Sure, I'd gladly
help cook our meal, if you'd sing along.'

The lady'd studied irony. 'No deals,
cricket. I beat metre right on the pots.'

The peeper fought off a *sanglot*. What was wrong
with play? Yes, the lady flayed off peels.
But weren't her pans a-boil dancing to *his* hots?

(A pennywhistle, Hohner made, in C.
Sweat and use have bared the brass about
the fingerholes. The whistle slit is bent
somewhat from an incisor's pressure. (We
remember in our heart of hearts the joy
of our first making noise. The girl or boy
in us will take the nuisance from a nephew
with a 'Let's see. I used to toot a few
tunes on one of these,' to find the digits
drop on the proper holes most handily,
lips fit themselves around that taste of tin.

And of course we blow it. The nephew's fidgets
are our own. Bird, we've never bin.
Our sisters holler: 'Give the kid his toy!'

(Things wear, and in the cosmic dream, we are
just things. So if our brass should show a bit,
we know what halting, hinted melodies
have blessed our knucklebones. The whistle's worn?

Then take up Lucy's skull (all could we find it),
size her to the slit. The tooth fits? Arh!
We wear her permanence, that we are born
to span meiosis' long antipodes.

Not that I'm Lucy, nor are you. Her sense
of music hits our sieves as leaky. What
she got from grass stalks as she plucked them twangs
useless when compared to Dvorák. By the jut
of her brow, however, let the moon's intense
remembering savannahs be her songs.

(To tell the whistle from the whistler's not
the point. Our hero has his mythic roots
in Hamelin. Doesn't care about the rats,
but *jeez!* to reel the children thru that knot
of timespace. Or just to jig himself, a*lone!*
In the mountain's very dark. The crystal mind
can hear perfection. Percolant, the mound
transforms the salty lattice of the bone.

(A wife of many foxtrots might just try:
'The whistler's hollow, not the whistle!' Song
isn't what she heard, or wanted to.
She's learned by heart her fables: Cricketry
can't cut it with the ants when winter's long
waltz wakens in the branches.

So ...)))))

I. *In which we set the passion in motion.*

An ordinary couple rises west
on Princess Street.
                        Twilight, of course.
                                    They stop
before a music store. He says, 'Let's just
have a look.' Not that he likes to Christmas shop.

An obvious beginning. (If I stress
that fables give up morals to who escape
this fading chasm between storefronts, neither's less.)
They stand, slightly apart, with the calm of a newsclip.

O 'cello, beyond that door, waiting to fall
into his arms (for those who don't), a sign
that reads:

> *Sorry, we're*
> CLOSED!

                        A hope at all
these days is fatal. Cancer is benign,
compared. Will a premonition, stall
his stepping in, refuse his hand! Decline!

2a. *In which we discover why the idea*
of the ghost of Marcel Proust reminiscing
on déjà vu *is so nostalgically sad.*

Missing the hubris cleanly as the probe
lifts away a layer of cortex, such
painless necessity at thirty-three
to fiddle himself silly.
If fatigue be that electrode in the lobe
opening on childhood's vestige, then its touch
is hollow without the presence: *how*
what's held, bottom between knees. 'Wow!'

sez a he, *circa* six, on the chair's
edge, unembarrassed as the tills ring.
Furtive gladness, by which they share
embrace, draws a simple song
out of body, his or its. Bare
wire joy thru this lobotomon.

2b.

Presumption like a stroll thru hell to draw
this proposition from the clay again:
Love. Will not stay in mind, this pain
adhering to the heart's visceral awe
of unrequited amness. Folks, the flaw
he's born to, solitary as the rain
that blinks thru blurring headlamps to the drain
and under, sings the trees to frenzy. Ah,

His Sysiphic corpse picks out a homeless
'April in Paris', but it's Christmas in Kingston.
Percussion's a chargeplate's click. Death soon
enough, when Hell's no surprise. Who will bless
this supplicant, who cares if it can be done?
April as longing, tho he's clumsy with the tune.

not 2b.

A man, he thinks the shoots are dainty that erupt
thru winter's matted carcass, can't conceive in thaw
the writhing of a lust which in his yard, abrupt
and noon by noon, entangles rotting up in raw.

A man remembers: as the carrion beetle moiled
beneath the haunch hide of some dog-killed critter, that
dead muscles seemed to ripple in a run, what soiled
the grass when beetle'd done can riddle tit for tat.

If seeing's not the heart, the sought (like simple joy
can bend preoccupation to obsession) still
eludes him: tendrilled thru the motor neuron's here
and now response to stimulus, his musings toy
with him, that he believe his longing be his will:
his nostrils flare, his blood beats bounty in his ear.

3. In which we are asked to assume a value for vivisection.

A rat hooked on the shock of pleasure starves.
The lab technician cleans the cage, zeroes
the counter, enters in the log heroes
by number, weight, and freedom that the wharves
will never hear of, pink-eyed troubadours
that improvised fate right on their brains. He shows
the kill to someone with a scalpel, mows
the skull fur off another batch. Remorse
can play no part in it. An unthot urge
is any cage the song itself declares
hunger's voice. Once feel the rubber glove
grasping the nape, the needle, then the surge
releasing perfect mercy, and the hairs
will stand stubbled in the skin for love.

4a.

Cheaper than a shrink and twice as light of
heart, sapmade maid, spright.
He was daft when he thot she was wooden; a daphne whose flight,
plied out to play (matching his clay) this plight of
transformation, one which wavered along a
random reconstruction of the song
all selfsick lovers claim makes two-edged wrong,
until they sense resistance to so strong a
desolated passion's less humane than
folding. At first she felt his fingers cramp,
but one morning she unbent his spine. A remaking gavotte,
droll and dolorous, see, such a comical man
burst green to his toetap, credulous the clamp
of his chest to heartwood, pumping as he ought.

4b.

Leaf lettuce and radishes. Beer. A breathy aroma
belched up the nose, noise for a May birthday.

                    er
              ov   the
            er   hill.
          ov   And
          er   she
Ov   lusty
virginal. Failing fire, she'll have a span
that'll give her to the hands of some unborn man.
Will she remember? Nights closed in her case
will his temporary fingers ghost again
down her tightened strings? O mortal 'cello!
At dawn, drowsy after play, he left her
on her side and went out to the porch. The maples dropped
flowerhusks among dried leaves. The soft
percussion tingled up his spine. Maples' grain
flamed in her ribs, an energy that's maple
fresh to the end, igniting dead men.

5. A monologue.

Fly me to the moon, and let us live
among the stars, our golden-appled, ceaseless
Eden. The trees blot out the better part
of heaven: to the south, ecliptic riven
by the buds, and to the north, Polaris
lost in dark branches. Cassiopeia's
M or W spells out a fate
ambiguous for either or the both of us.

On second thot, how would we manage airsuits,
solar radiation, plastic dome
with therapeutic murals of a home
we would grow sick for. We'd become two brutes
without a tune, until we understood
just what beneath the varnish marks the wood.

6a.

How *duz* he give up jealousy and doubt?
Both virgin in a sense (he's had no fresher
'cello; fervent, she's dallied, true, but only
in the shop), they've neither really learned to string
the other, *obbligato*, 'long. The song
in seed has many versions; of the best
are those that draw such *tremolo* to rest.

It isn't that he's looking for an out;
really, his sense of timing wants to mesh her
tensions thru his cardial cordage. Lonely
as his solo's been, he'd grasp the sting
sheathed by desire, and pull. Is it so wrong
that as he holds her throbbing to his chest,
her tickle be his heart's discord's arrest?

6b.

Would she regret a man so set? (The habit
was an alms from Pavlov's acolytes,
but our ex-inmate chafed beneath the misfit.
Confessor Skinner's kid'd showed him his rites.
'Behaviour mod or pentagrams,' *she'd whispered,*
'nothing holds the changeling but belief.
Escape is giving up.' *Her answer festered
where the seams had welted to relief.*)

The calloused pads his tips are generating
are what embryonic ease secretes.
Today. Toward her.
            Still, stale crosshatching
on his shoulders stitches if he lurch.
Sweat's salt on his back; out of his hairshirt,
the horse's asshair tightens his release.

7. In which we consider some popular clichés.

Some clothes don't make the man unless they're worn
with clear intent, heart velcroed to a sleeve
or jockstrapped balls, to understate the pose.

These wetsuits that we're issued when we're born
will clad our asses as we take our leave,
their threads picked for reweaving. So it goes.

You know that bit about fragments of Caesar
sifting thru the ages to be us?
Particulate Vlad Tepes we forget.

(Oh, since he got his babe, he likes to squeeze 'er
day in, night out. He kicks up such a fuss,
you'd think he'd *made* the atoms that beget

such helices of passion.) A dust clings
naked to his fingers from her strings.

8.

But who *is* he, fellow creature, to get the rush
like *I* do? Binged prodigious by desire,
has he become more gullible or wiser
or does he even wonder which is which?

Forgive the speculation. *I* must admit
he's somewhat identical. Post-modern crit
has made it hard to just prioritize
one's passions. Worst that can happen is, you size

this sucker up, and you get bored. So what?
You've lived this or not. If you decide
he can invent the plot from what you hide,
you keep on reading. If you don't, he dies.
Nice and simple. Meanwhile, 'I' relies
on grammar, *Oxford*, and the butt of 'but'.

9.

If he were some gorilla (Koko *is:*
'Fine animal *me!*' signed in Ameslan)
he'd never think arpeggios. A man,
amen, whose agent, *I*, the cosmic whiz-
kid (yourself not) weighs the moral biz-
ness he commits and lets you test the plan
he lives extemporaneous. His clan
is voiced, urbane and canny.
                              Quick, a quiz:

What ape called *Pan* has ever wailed on pipes?
What capuchin has ever flailed a bow?
What nude primate in the shower's *not*
been tempted by acoustics to draw gripes
from mothers-in-law in earshot? Did he know
th'impediments his baboon yodel'd brought?

10a. *In which we argue that age and experience are equally confusing to the neophyte.*

'You won't get far without a teacher,' Ibi
told me, after she'd found out how much.
'That's him,' I thot, *'another me more lucky,*
fungoing gospel freely in the clutch.'

I phoned.
       I left a message.
              Noon, he called,
distant, insistent that I hear him play.
'Okay.' 'Then four tomorrow, under Chown Hall.'
The other end went empty. Did I say

four sharp? A sense of fairness down to his
mechanical pencil, which he first of all
flourished to forestall opening his case

and glom his lovely strongly by her neck.
My jaw apparently unhinged. The effect
rattled him. He asked about my taste.

10b.

He played a piece from Schumann. He played well.
That is, he read the music, didn't stumble
once, and seemed to *feel*. He sat. I rumbled
up a C scale, made the tonic swell.
He sighed, 'You're very Wagner.' I replied,
'A brother more to Hindemith, perhaps.'
He frowned, 'What do you know of Starker?' Gaps
abyssed me. 'Technique's everything,' I lied.

'Not everything,' he smiled. 'Your 'cello's German.'
I doubletook, 'The accent's that pronounced?'
but I confess my heart went bump. The lull
ticked on, and, ready to endure the sermon –
miscegenation, Magyars, muck – I glanced
at him. 'My wife plays flute,' he coughed. My pal.

II.

We grip each other, freshly anxious, as tho we'd
read from a tantric text. Our ease upended.

Do the first eight bars. Repeat.
                                        But
after half an hour, I chuck the bow
and go into *Willow, Weep for Me*. Willow,
weep. You feel manipulated, freeze.

Debonair, I ramble till I notice,
pull back and touch the graining of the spruce
over your belly.   'Wait.   Don't.   Whatever
the mistake, it's mine. One wood to another,

I forget sometimes the fix I'm in.
Tinder for old flames. I'd gladly split
kindling from my arm if it would bring
clean conflagration with it.'

12.

We've practised. We've perfected. Now we wait
outside a soundproof cubicle, wherein there strains
and puffs his 'nother dupe thru Popper's scales,
tsk, emulating Janos' breathy Bach.

A well-used Heintzmann stands against the wall,
the keyboard open, anybody's slut.
I check your case's clips, and wander west
and look, and shyly plunk a couple chords.

The door dechuffs, a smell of locker room
and rosin; Starker manqué trundles forth.

The voice within pronounces, severed head,
'That rondo needs more work,' and we are next.

We start. 'Your A's flat,' and those hands reach out
to tune the string that in disgust you snap.

13.

A Bach transcription for beginner.
                                        Practice
isn't the harmony
                        is fingers and strings straining
together. Is we here, animate. '*Saw,*
saw,' caws Alex. 'Keep it balanced
on the *next* note!'
                        One part wood
and one *tired* arm.
                                'Don't clench. Relaxed,
but focused.'
                        Sure. Squeeze a pure tone
from finger's aching.
                                A flutter on an open
string.
            '*That* isn't music!' he yelps.

But Alex, the world doesn't have perfect parts.
Hell lied. Nothing follows except
belief,
            looser than the last best
shirt,
            its back
                        slit.

14. *In which the persona narrating talks to his better part.*

Another me more lucky? Who was I,
think, kidding, friend? A fate diverges?
A crotched witching switch tickles the source
and one end evolves angels wholesale?
Give me a break, a break. Think of your *ka*,
think placenta, pal, your organ twin
dead at birth, think caul, dried and put
aside, sprinkled in your tea at thirty,
oh, think, sweet jésu, joy of man's desiring,
of happiness. Just happiness. Just song.

I took her to me wholly, holy, lone
and weary, rock me in the bosom, bub,
that while I groan these midwife lullabies,
her belly varnish dimly mirrors lies.

15a.

We marry whom we marry, and they bring
their chattels, cattle, kin, their plague of flies
emmaggoting the dung to make the sting
until the iridescence of those eyes
becomes the meat we lay ourselves beside.

Our lovers, teachers, gurus, masters, gods
begin to crumble as we touch them, hide
their sores from us, alarmed, despite the odds
that we will surely ogle our corrupt
urges reflected in their oiled skins.

Our brides daub rouge on faces that erupt
with ulcers of our most unconscious sins
until our crones croon songs of clever hooks
to hold our mouths set right, morticians' tricks.

15b.

We marry whom we marry and we bring
along with our complaints, our smelly parts
and irritating habits, that which starts
to question, first ironic, just what thing
we've brought upon ourselves, but, growing used
to its perception of disaster, nags,
more earnestly, how obvious the snags
we trip on; grows withdrawn, blackly amused.

If single-minded impulse twists our fates
in filaments of exile thru our cells
and makes us *each*, this *other* so appals
our nose for justice that we balk. It baits
us with its greener grass, it saddles, sells
its load of goods on us, which burden *galls!*

16a. *In which we extend the figure into another confusing subplot.*

The dream-wraith, he of the road to Emmaus,
stares over your left shoulder, understudy
to your furtive life, your bathroom thots.
See him in the mirror as you brush
your pearly whites? *He knows what you are thinking!*
Make no mistake; he isn't out to get you.
He's waiting for the stunt that you pass on,
the semi-fatal slip that clicks the latch
behind you in the dark. And while you grope
toward the monster you imagine, masked
he acts as you would for the camera's eye.
As you come to, his latex has no pores.
Remove that skin with caution: Lucy's skull
smiles beside you, amorous, on the pillow.

16b.

'More flies with honey' is his motto, shield
a field sable, crowned with noumenon.
Stitched on his colours, Gothic blackface, bronze
above brass studs: 𝔗𝔥𝔢 𝔎𝔦𝔡; sealed
in leathern black, his shanks, his thighs, his cod;
and in the smoke and beerhaze holds his vigil,
armed with his lance of eighteen ounces, cudgel
against fate and bullshit: scourge of God.

Not errant, he, so much as ignorant
that armies clash and stumble thru the gore and
shit to touch the Grail. Against the wackoes
stoned at the bar, his Childe-like purpose echoes
virtuously sly, a blank fiat:

'I tot I taw a big, bad puddy tat!'

16c.

Sweet Tweety! How an emblem's innocence
Quarles with nothing blander than his spoke
upon the wheel. Turn, Great Being, sense
the cataclysms that inform his stroke
as it presses stripes into the pockets.
No *soft* love. Nothing down a notch from brute
purity in animation. *Fuck it*'s
oathed in spades for anything that's cute.

The sharply flinty pathway of his soul
let him march unshod, his guerdon whole
before him at a zenith, winking at-
mospheric; let forking synchronicity bat
ambiguous two fifty; bring in the clowns
to play the outfield. Life has its ups and downs.

16d.

His leather hand rests on her shoulder, idly
stroking the bare wood. 'I sleep,' I say
to no one who will listen, but for you.
Help me. Stop him. She will not. Her fear
is charged with an intoxication, id-like,
feeding her adrenaline. *Sagst
mir, 'Wachst du,' Doktor Jung.* And breathe that *du*
upon my heart to ease the dread I fare.

I set ourselves a simple goal when we
began: to have it all, the evil, good,
the vast indifference below the thrones
of either, where our deepest dreaming drones
inaudible. Stroking the bare wood,
his leather hand rests on her shoulder, idly.

16e. *In which we consider seriously the cat's options.*

The knack of peeling layers from the plies
that bind us comes of scrutinizing ties
along an often sauntered stretch of track;
that regularity at twilight tricks
a hobbled stride into believing pliés
motor an approaching dark, and tease
a sense of balance that inclines the trek
toward a sudden, blinding orb, the trucks'
steel screeching on the rails, while, enervate
with terror, legs refuse to break the pattern
and just do their stuff, like, fade, rather than
play out this little nightmare. It's too late
to think Sylvester's feigned panache will tide
you when the you-faced phantoms want your hide.

16f.

Well, heart, you dirty rat, you've snookered me,
passing an easy shot to shut me out.
Two banks at least, a charybdis and skill
ah don't possess, more English than ah kin.

Slow diastole of hope, it's time to see
The Kid for what he is, and that his clout
pfaffs silly at the sphinxling that will kill
machismo where it stands. But for the din

(ah, soft, so soft) of ivorine on felt,
his concentration hears no consonant
reminder that the table may contain
within lozenged mahogany what's dealt
so flatly otherwith: the sycophant
his doppelgänger, cueless, must remain.

16g.

Double's double, toil and trouble has he
plenty, keeping up the wherewithal this circus
needs to run. 𝕿𝖍𝖊 𝕶𝖎𝖉 would not admit relation.
Squinting past the cueball, the desperado
(inherent in the stance) will not believe
this trance is brought to you by paycheque. Folks,
let's hear it for the man behind the scenes
who pays the rent and schlepps. His daily scrapes
with peanut butter and soiled diapers posits
his wider worth.
                    Stand up there, *haus*fraud, take
a bow. Yes, he's our angel, friends, a fruit
of the loom seraph at the bathroom sink
calmly drawing half a glass of water
in plastic tumbler to hand a sleepy child.

17a.

A mentor can admonish for so long
as he convinces us he's not the jerk
we guessed, practised, yes, but just as wrong
about his own rehearsal of the murk.
Gesang, wie du ihn lehrst, ist nicht Begehr,
wrote Rilke, Alex.
              (But does anyone re*mem*ber
how that shaft of light is found? Where,
before we dug us down, another temper
altogether jerked these strings?
                        (What badass
boys we are, groping in the silk.))

Love's no number.
Pythagoras
and Lawrence Welk
cringe before her.

17b.

As the presence of the fly is one
damnation (Beelzebub's an entity
has worn his share of shirts), so anguish is.
Better to have been consumed. Dear Alex,
the fly of the house, the winter fly, is dying
and it does not buzz anguish. Only we.

Buzz off. True, when she fixed on you, I saw
a profile hinting at the gorgon. Wires.

But the *need. You* think that what you're playing
is a *chello.*   No   no   no.
Audience orientation and seat politics
bore love stiff. Alex, I'd give
you money to teach me and shut up, only,
when I hold her, now, against my chest,
her tuning's out. Just out. I can't adjust it.

17c.

Such jitters jealousy will sic on us!
An accidental meeting in the music
library, but he's helpful with a problem.
Two students giggle over *Lohengren,* earphones
snapped on. Ibi'd said his concert was
accomplished. Yes, there's some embarrassment,
a finger pulled too quickly on a line
of sixteenth notes: he asks me what I'm playing:
'Fly Me to the Moon': his smile returns
awry: I ask him: Kodály.   I say:
'My wife once swam with him. She was in grade
school. He was almost seventy. The same
pool, you understand.' I ask if he knows
who might have composed 'Fly Me to the Moon'.

18. *In which we return to the farce.*

Spring came to Hell, but held one bud secret.
Her heart, or really, her psychosocial affect.

Statistics don't apply to horticulture
purgatorial, but her penchant to alter
experimental data did distort results.

Hell fumed. How were the stiffs to run the maze
if they kept getting lost in holidays
from concentration. Hell rumbled thru its faults.

The scientific method has its trouble
measuring a lesion made by joy.
Morbidity is evident, but a scalpel
fine enough evades technology.

Hell called up Heisenberg. *'Uncertainty
is freedom!'* whined that phantom untherely.

19a.

Confusions falter to confessions, cues
get blown. An offbeat snags me unawares
partway thru a phrase. I stumble, lose
the sense. Pretence assumes a face, and stares:

'Well, Pablo? Demons aren't your only flaw.
The ringing in your ears as we guffaw
should really clue you in. Your sin's a lack,
the unavoidable omission, Jack.'

A sourness squats in my expectancy.
No, I can't take such cranky information.
A hope is all I got. Can I forget
the scheming of that slapstick ecstasy
as Daffy smooches wetly Elmer's noggin?
'Woo, woo! Woo, woo!'   You bet.

19b.

Elmer Fudd, cherubic with a shotgun,
blooms his eros substitution out.
Daffy scatters to regroup a clout
that bends both barrels back. If Daffy got one

thru the heart, would Fudd's cupidity
for duckmeat make him pluck the quacker? No.
Sentimental Elmer'd give a show
of grief that would transcend stupidity.

The leap from Saturday TV to passion
isn't so farfetched as you might guess.
What keeps us banging at the obvious
is just that bald appraisal of the ration
love *does* stick in our gullets, so unless
that's a ducksuit, bud, this *could* get serious.

20. *In which we place a mother-in-law in historical perspective.*

Ibi
was right.
Vanity is what.
'Vain' she calls me
her *w* on the tip
of her tongue. Karzag bred her,
Budapest offered her opera. The law's mother
who plays piano, morose deceased Austrians let slip
from under her fingers to trouble our respective pasts.

But that selfsame love burning frenzy thru the bush lasts
beyond its own consumption, *anyu.* We inherit ashes. What *we* keep
rubbing against, a name or quirk, ignites perplexity, this need to
    keen.
Vain that an accent elongates the pause. If chances for reproaches
    grow lean,
like old-world workmanship in craft-happy Canada, how to bridge
    the gulf? Just

leap!

21a. *A critical aside.*

There rose a tree; its branches were all wood,
whose leaves ate sun as gracefully as air
had borne the risings and the settings. Bare
in its grain, each wood shone. And breath was good.

The song has been and will be and all is
where suckle roots, and springs that joyous grief
within earth's sandy lattice, when each leaf
dies to its heart to hume an interstice.

O, 'cello, risen out of planks, the tree
must *flow*er! Hold me, have my fingers take
the bow so lightly, lightly, death won't hear
us as we hum. The moon's bare face first taught
your wood self exhalation, 'cello; free
us from its grin; let our ingraining make
the mortal of us grow beyond our fear.

21b.

Did Wagner foretell Adolf? Did the man
whose Christmas present to his wife recalls
some long-lost sadness in my three-year-old
presage a sense of kinship with the Rat?

He wasn't fond of Semites; to be fair,
he doesn't seem to've esteemed Prussians either.
He never wrote a goodly piece for 'cello.
He never held a muzzle to a neck.

His *Ring* did nostradamus to young Eichmann
or Göbbels or whoever had the balls
that needed clipping long before the gold
was melted down and soap made from the fat.

His farts were not recorded? What the heck,
to clear the air, let the poor bugger go!

*Cher*man is a tongue we should've learned
from *Hogan's Heroes* or from Vonnegut.
Billy Pilgrim's take on what got burned
at least preserved some irony. Ah, but

Bayreuth *can* hold a candle to the Met.
Just don't ask what it's made of. One pure tone
arising from that pit is good to set
the whole enclosure shivering in the bone.

A grainy shot of Adolf, leaning forward,
right hand extended, mouth agape on something,
perhaps a photo of a rare performance,
the Leader singing *Lieder* (eyes cast shoreward?
Frisch weht der Wind?), his posture come a dumb thing
on the page to magnify abhorrence?

21d.

Treblinka's twitchy tremor thru the soul
(doesn't that sound tactful?) left us self-shocked.
Of course, we blamed the Nazis, but we knew
the time's spasmodic eyeblink'd thrown us all
against the cosmos' retina, and tho
from our perspective we can tell the white
hat from the black ('Hi ho, Silver!'), we feel
unclean. Hippocrates, what purgative?
Infuse a hellebore the time provides:

This little analyst was Swiss, and this
a Viennese Jew. This one was terrified
of rats, and this some sort of socialist.
This little one sat in a box that trapped
orgone, orgone, orgone, all day long.

22a. *In which we wind things up to wind things down.*

The night you pointed out that true and false
prove each other's backsides, I refused.
'Anthropomorphization,' I shouted, 'only
goes so far! You are a *thing*, you tool!'

We sulked another seven bars of Ives
before I caught up with the punchline. Who
seems to ogle the face of stuff may have
another set of cheeks in mind. ''Cello,'

I sighed, 'this dirty talk is really mine.
If the shirt fits, that's because I wear it.
Threadbare fibres galvanize the tissue

culture. The choices machine me to a slaver.
Taste. Hell help me if I am to escape
that aggravating clang's loose drool.'

22b.

Comes a time the joke shows its bum stung
from the slapstick. So this *was* a one-notion stand,
this *in*post of bewilderment among
idea's crews, a burdened ampersand
that tried to tie loose ends. Overrun.
What we wanted was the Amazon
to *re*perceive or Stevie Wonder's loud
blindness blessing a first Homeric crowd.

The banal takes a swack at our version. Steve's shades
would simply drag the darkness thru whatever
vision we pretended. Days on the river
would never get us to the other side.

Hell, darling, beckons, as I turn
away or back. So what? Both choices burn.

22c.

Wood of my bone, the whole act's clearly
dildoed, axe and axeman taking it in
the ear. Dear, dear apparatus, we
wail it, wiled, in sin. Varnish and skin
are fallacies of mutual sublimation.
Who'll believe it, our ungrounded love? Re-
viewers? Voyeurs? Thing, the dedication
those well-loved many want as necessary.

Cripes, it was only supposed to be fun, a few
daily tickles up the fingerboard, some blues
to rinse out sanity, that sort of stuff.

Enough! Whining's not how we'll make it whole.
Cold showers. Push-ups. An hour's torture, solo bow.
Virtuosity because it's tough!

22d.

The path from Hell is paved with good intent.
Those gritty promises beneath your feet
aren't crushed, just crazed from weeping and the heat.
Behind you in the shadows, breath is pent
against the moment that the cool, moist air
of ordinary night revitalize
who follows.
              Stars! Above you!

                          Don't chastise
your longing; it was pure. Absolve despair,
that served you faithfully. Its stunted limbs
embraced your harp as, kneeling on the crag
your life had come, you witnessed that first hag,
her lips bespittled, gut your sacred hymns.

Damn only with what ease the flints could part
the strangled cage your ribs made for your heart.

22e. *In which the old man gets drunk again.*

Hell's that portion of the heart engenders
monsters; loving Lucy in the dreamtime
didn't seem to lead to this. The benders,
purgative at first, enhanced the deathmime

backlit on a skin that, cured and scraped,
resembled lampshade stretched across the cave's
one exit. Ma'am, we kept them till they aped
a natural civility, then waved

them off, and heard them shouting in the distance
obscene understandings of their parents.

My bride and I made toil and lust, this dance
we dance (it's very old). We hung up *daren'ts*
on the tree, wiped their asses, fed them....

Lady, free us now, lest we outlive them.

22f.

If thot be hindsight *a priori*, think
divergence, to and from, this moment's nub.

Love's delirious solipsism, bub,
is hanging on an exponential brink:
what if the might-have-been were akshoolized
and, *deus ex machina*, let this 'I'
retake the basic cream of pie in sky
right on the shnozz again, he'd get some wised
up, but that to fake the outcome, fate
still plays the odds on even, and the gate
still takes the ball at random. Trust will map
the *terra incognita* of some trap
sick heart, sick mind, sick spirit won't deny.

Now 'I' will suck some tailpipe truth and die.

22g.

To say this equals that, or something's like,
where does it get us, really? Mary pisses
in the hall. Otherwise, the ward is calm.
He sleeps naked. The nurse with the light goes 'Yike!'
in the night when he seems not to wake. There be abysses
who speak in the duct's hiss, clear, a balm.

A 'cello's grief, and love is madness. Verb
whose tautological inheritance
has led thy parents in a merry dance,
didsdoo expect this would be a blurb

to win them over? Laugh, chicky, laugh; it's just
as good as crying.

          Right. Carol hight
this nurse who sits beside him. So we might
live without thee, *Maya*, if we must.

23. *His confession.*

'Looking back, I see I should have told you
you only wanted to be happy. I, of course, too
morally double-jointed in this celebration
of loose bearings, ethical magnetic shift,
but somehow happy didn't equal well fed.
Or well shagged or blotto. When the wheel
spins, we go up and we come down. Looks
like the same place. If *you* don't get off here
don't tell *me* to. Cynicism's *de rigueur*
only in that it's *lingua franca*. Define love,
quickly, in twenty-five failures or less.
I might as well have stuffed it in your psyche
for all the understanding we either got.
Hello?

       Are you still …?'

24. *Exeunt omnes.*

'Cello:

    When you read this note, I'm gone.
The X-ray showed my heart intact, but with
a stethoscope, the murmur is apparent.
You'll get custody of bow and rosin.
Although it's in my power to bequeath
a meaty dissolution, your hope's transparent.

P.S. If you should try to find me, speak
first to our keepers. I'm bunked with an old piano.
The scratches she's acquired have given her
a scale that helps us sort the hurting out.
It's not so bad. We play around the squeak
she picked up in her baser tones, even tho
the resonations keep us somewhat unsure.
But it's a start, we feel. We share the rent.

) *An Envoi*

'These fourteen lines. These weeks. This life.' 'How awk

word,' crow alone replies.

Wayne Clifford's debut collection of poems *Man In A Window* (1965) was the first book to be published by Stan Bevington's fledgling Coach House Press. Clifford was one of Coach House's early manuscript editors, and acquired books by Michael Ondaatje, George Bowering and bpNichol, among others.

Clifford has not published a trade book since *An Ache in the Ear* in 1979. He was working on a poetry collaboration with bpNichol at the time of Nichol's death in 1988, and continues to refine and expand *From Exile*, a massive sequence of some 360 sonnets.

The owner of about twenty-five musical instruments, including a number that he designed himself, Clifford plays weekly in an amateur jazz band.

An earlier, shorter version of *On Abducting the 'Cello* appeared as a *Front* chapbook in 1988.

A section of the Prologue appeared in *Quarry*.

Thanks to Mary Joan Edwards for initial keyboarding and formatting, and the many insightful discussions, and to the many who have read draft versions and commented.